What do you see on this milkweed leaf? It looks like a little jellybean, or a dewdrop. But come closer and you'll find that it's really an egg. And something alive is hidden inside.

This is how big the egg really is.

Soon the egg is ready to hatch. A tiny body squiggles and wiggles its way out. Do you know what it is? It's a caterpillar! And it's VERY, VERY HUNGRY!

This is how big the baby caterpillar is.
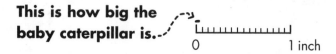
0   1 inch

Right away, the caterpillar eats its eggshell. Then it begins to nibble leaves. It eats and eats, growing bigger and fatter. And as it grows, it changes. Now the caterpillar has velvety stripes.

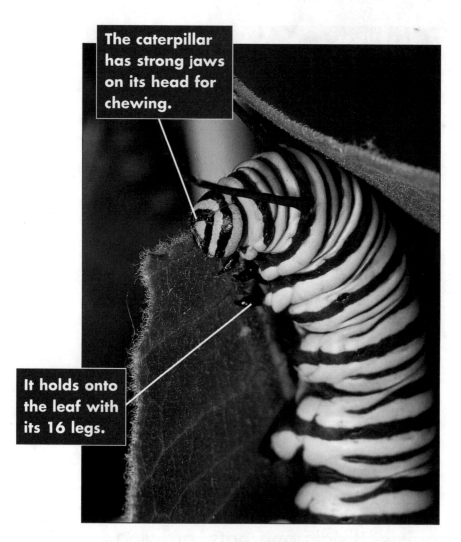

The caterpillar has strong jaws on its head for chewing.

It holds onto the leaf with its 16 legs.

Munch! Crunch! The caterpillar is an eating machine! It moves along the milkweed plant, chewing up the leaves.

When it is about 10 days old, the caterpillar stops eating. It looks for a safe place to rest.

This is how big the caterpillar is now.

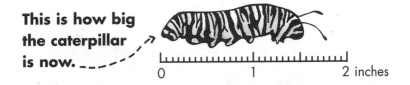

0   1   2 inches

What letter of the alphabet do you think the caterpillar looks like?

The caterpillar crawls under a leaf and hangs upside down. Then something amazing happens. The caterpillar begins to change shape!

The caterpillar has become a chrysalis! Inside the chrysalis, incredible things are happening. Nature is putting on a kind of magic show. It is turning the caterpillar into something new!

One week later, you can see what's inside the chrysalis. And it is just starting to come out. It pushes and pushes until the chrysalis splits. Look! A beautiful monarch butterfly!

Can you see the monarch's wings inside the chrysalis?

The monarch's head pokes out of the chrysalis shell first.

The butterfly only has six legs now, but it has grown brand new wings. At first, they are wet and crumpled. Slowly, the butterfly stretches them out.

The monarch hangs onto the shell to stretch its wings.

How long does it take the monarch to break out of the shell and stretch its wings?

The monarch rests and lets its wings dry in the sun. All the velvet stripes are gone now. Instead, the butterfly is covered with tiny scales.

This is how big the butterfly is.

0   1   2   3   4 $4\frac{1}{2}$ inches

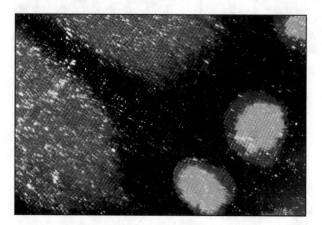

Take a close look at the monarch's wing. Tiny scales give the butterfly its color and pattern.

Soon the butterfly can fly. It flutters from flower to flower. The butterfly has a straw-like tube on its head. It pokes the tube into a blossom to sip nectar. Nectar is a butterfly's food.

You can find butterflies wherever there are flowers. There are 12 butterflies fluttering in this garden. How many monarchs can you count?

Monarchs are poisonous. Their bright colors warn birds and other animals to stay away. They say, "Don't eat me. I taste awful!"

As soon as there's a nip in the air, monarchs do what many birds do. They fly south for the winter. On wings as thin as tissue paper, they can fly across the ocean!

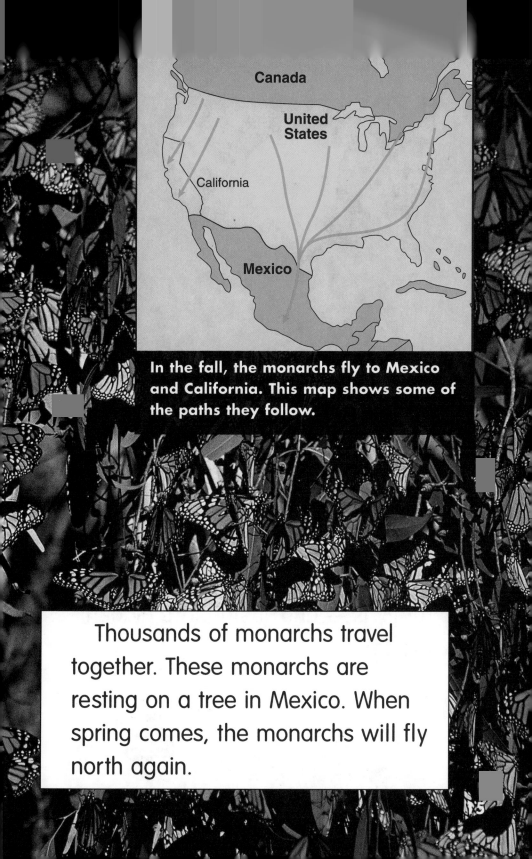

Canada

United States

California

Mexico

In the fall, the monarchs fly to Mexico and California. This map shows some of the paths they follow.

Thousands of monarchs travel together. These monarchs are resting on a tree in Mexico. When spring comes, the monarchs will fly north again.

On the way home, a monarch drops something on a milkweed leaf. It looks like a little jellybean, or a dewdrop. But <u>you</u> know what it really is — and just what's hidden inside!